Caroline M. Bell

(1874-1970)

And

The Peconic Bay Impressionists

COVER:
View of Rocky Neck, Gloucester, ca. 1925

INSIDE FRONT AND END LEAFS:
Winter Day, Cutchogue, 1917

Published in the United States of America in 2006 by
M.T. Fine Arts, Inc./Wallace Gallery, 37A Main Street, East Hampton, New York 11937
Tel. (631) 329-4516 Fax. (631) 329-4517
E mail: wallacearts@earthlink.net
Web site: www.artnet.com/wallace.html

Library of Congress Card Number ISBN 0-9787378-0-6

Photography by Tim Lee
Printed by Pine Barrens Printing, Westhampton, NY

This volume has been published in conjunction with the exhibition "Caroline M. Bell and The Peconic Bay Impressionists".

Wallace Gallery
October 24, 2006-December 3, 2006

Suffolk County Historical Society
December 8, 2006-April 30, 2007

Caroline M. Bell

(1874-1970)

And

The Peconic Bay Impressionists

Terry Wallace

Forward

The *Peconic School* has long been thought as being comprised of a handful of National Academicians - Irving Wiles, Edward August Bell, Henry and Edith Mitchill Prellwitz and less known artists like Charles Bittinger and Orlando Rouland. These artists formed the nucleus of the *Peconic Art Colony*, living in an area known as Indian Neck, Peconic, Long Island.

Despite the popularity of these artists, who at times commanded national attention, another group of artists who I refer to as the *Peconic Bay Impressionists* led by Caroline M. Bell was working in the small hamlets dotting the North Fork.

These two groups of artists did not mingle very often. At times, members of either group shared ideas with one another at each other's studios. Sometimes these artists gathered together at music recitals. On at least three occasions, artists from the *Peconic Colony* and members of the *Peconic Bay Impressionists* exhibited their work together. The first of these exhibitions was in 1913 to support Eastern Long Island Hospital. A second exhibition took place in 1934, sponsored by the North Fork Art Club in Riverhead. The last exhibition was at the Southold Tercentenary Exhibition in 1940, when Southold Town celebrated its 300 year anniversary. Like good neighbors, these two groups of artists came together when the community was in need.

Stylistically and educationally, the *Peconic Colony* artists and the *Peconic Bay Impressionists* shared very little. On one hand, the *Peconic Colony* artists led by Irving Wiles were educated at the National Academy of Design. Their teachers were artists who trained their students in a conventional manner, following a fixed formula in their paintings. And, as artists who were educated at the National Academy they became accustomed to exhibiting at major exhibitions. These artists moved to the Peconic region of Long Island from large cities like New York or Washington, D.C. At times, members of this group enjoyed a celebrity-like status.

On the other hand, Caroline M. Bell and many of the *Peconic Bay Impressionists* were taught by a different group of artists. These included Birge Harrison, John F. Carlson, Emile Gruppe and Anthony Thieme.   Although some of these men had been educated at the National Academy, they guided their students in individual expression and technique. Their emphasis in teaching dealt with the fundamental principles of design and composition in picture-making as applied to the practical problems of out-door painting.

Unlike the artists of the *Peconic Colony* who had settled in Indian Neck, Caroline M. Bell and the *Peconic Bay Impressionists* often painted together as a group. They painted along Peconic Bay on both sides of Long Island. They also traveled to other parts of New York State and to New England where they painted at Rockport and Gloucester, Massachusetts. Here, they often became members of important art organizations and participated together in painting exhibitions.

Bell and the *Peconic Bay Impressionists* had another major difference from their counterparts—most of these artists were born and bred on the North Fork of Long Island. In fact, many of their forefathers, including Bell's were the founding fathers of Southold Town.

Sometime during the late 1980's, I purchased my first painting by Caroline Bell from an antique store in Mattituck. I immediately began making inquiries about the artist because I recognized the work as that of someone who appeared to be trained by a competent impressionist painter. In the following years, I began purchasing as many paintings as I could locate in antique stores, yard sales or auctions. In the beginning, the names--Wickham, Hawkins, McAdams, Wells, Moore, Howard, Raynor, Howell, Young, Kurth, Bassarear, Kroeger, Mothersele and others meant very little to me. There was scant information I could find on these artists, so I began visiting all of the cemeteries on the North Fork of Long Island. There I found the birth and death dates for most of the artists who had painted the pictures I had in my possession. Then through further research, I learned about Caroline "Dolly" Bell and her influence on the *Peconic Bay Impressionists*.

This catalogue would not be complete if I did not mention several people who have shared an interest in this group of artists and their desire to bring their stories to light. John Kramer and Geoffrey Fleming of the Southold Historical Society, Ron Edeen, John Crimmins, Dennis Hodges and Andrew Nimmo, collectors/dealers who have helped promote this school, William Robinson, dealer and early collector, Henry Broegge, auctioneer and owner of South Bay Auctions and author John Esten who has written extensively about Long Island art history. Additionally, I would like to thank Jeffrey Walden of the Mattituck-Laurel Public Library, Susan Bergmann of the Riverhead Public Library, Mariella Ostroski of the Cutchogue–New Suffolk Free Library and Norman Wamback, President of the Mattituck Historical Society for their help in this project. A prayer of thanks to the late Carleton Kelsey, former East Hampton Town Historian and Amagansett Librarian for his help in cataloging paintings by Caroline Bell which were rendered in Amagansett.

I owe a debt of gratitude to Mattituck resident Ray Nine for his sharing personal knowledge and photographs of Caroline Bell with me. A similar debt of thanks is owed to Mark and Ann Gaynor for their warm hospitality and information about Helen Kroeger and Otto Kurth. Much appreciation to Gertrude Ali, daughter of Agnes J. Mothersele for her help in identifying photographs and providing paintings needed for this catalogue. I am indebted to artists George McAdams (age 100) and Larry Waitz (age 96) for the invaluable information they shared with me as well as to Bob Kuhne, President of the Old Town Arts & Crafts Guild. George Hallock, IV deserves mention for his sharing personal knowledge about his father, George Hallock, Jr. with me. I would also like to thank Joan Kaelin McNulty who shared information about her father, John Kaelin and Fred Miner who shared stories about his father, Gilbert B. Miner. Telephone calls to former Mattituck librarian and Caroline Bell biographer, Alice Rosenfeld provided information toward this catalogue that is greatly appreciated.

I would like to thank Wally Broege and the staff of the Suffolk County Historical Society and Keri Lamparter of Lamparter Communications. Further thanks to my assistant Clarebeth Cunningham and to Nancy Flesch, Matt Egan and John Pasqualicchio of Pine Barrens Printing.

Peter Hastings Falk deserves a special mention for his insight in this endeavor.

Last, I would like to thank my wife Melissa for her assistance and support throughout this undertaking. A commentary that I hope will create public awareness for the *Peconic Bay Impressionists*, as this group of artists deserves recognition and further scholarship.

Terry Wallace
June 2006

Photograph of Caroline M. Bell (standing) and Julia Wickam, circa 1900.
(Courtesy of the Southold Historical Society)

Caroline M. Bell

(1874-1970)
A Peconic Bay Impressionist and Her Vision of Nature

Caroline M. Bell or "Dolly" as she was known was an important impressionist painter and influential teacher to many artists who lived on the North Fork of Long Island. Bell was living (at least part-time) in the Peconic region of Long Island when Irving Wiles (1861-1948), Edward August Bell (1862-1953) (no relation), Henry (1865-1940) and Edith Mitchill Prellwitz (1865-1944) and a small group of other academically trained artists were settling into Indian Neck, Peconic.

Caroline Bell was born on September 1, 1874 to Jackson Wood Bell and Letitia Vandervoort Bell (1837-1907). Her parents were socially prominent and wealthy. Her grandfather was Henry Vandervoort, the Clerk of the Court of Sessions of New York. Her grandmother was Susan Osborn, a relative of William Purrier, one of the original settlers of Southold Town and through her descendants Bell was related to the Reeves, Tuthills, Hortons and Goldsmith families of the North Fork.[1] These were the names of the founding families of Southold Town, the oldest township on Long Island.

Caroline's parents separated when she was a child. She began spending summers with her mother at the family homestead. Later, she rented rooms at the *Brooklyn* from a relative, Herbert Conkling (1857-1935).[2] Also known as the Octagon House, this building still stands at the corner of Love Lane and Route 25A in Mattituck. Eventually, Bell built a home and studio near Love Lane and Sound Avenue in Mattituck, overlooking a creek to Mattituck Inlet. Here she acquired the nickname "Dolly" and began taking students and entertaining other artists.

Bell's interest in the arts began as a young woman. The earliest information found about her is from an article in the Brooklyn Eagle on September 11, 1887, "Caroline Bell is playing Mrs. George Hearne in the play, *"Seldom What They Seem."*[3] George Hearne was a philanthropist and one of the most important art collectors in America at the end of the nineteenth century. Apparently, Bell was interested in becoming an actress, her role as George Hearne's wife.

A person of means, Bell may have attended a college or university as a young woman. However, it is unknown at this time what her academic background was.

While there is little doubt Caroline M. Bell was a trained painter, there is no specific record of her studying with any artist in particular. However, it is believed she began her studies with (Lovell) Birge Harrison (1854-1929) in Woodstock, New York as she began to visit this part of New York State with the Reeves family as a young woman.4. Her cousin

Figure 1- Birge Harrison, *The Artists Farm, Woodstock, N.Y.* oil on board, 18 ½ x 23 in.

George Reeve, an aspiring artist exhibited at the Art Exhibition for the Benefit of Eastern Long Island Hospital in 1913.

Birge Harrison founded the Art Students League Summer School in Woodstock, New York in 1897. The school became so popular it attracted many students, eventually turning Woodstock into an artist colony. Harrison is best known for his atmospheric landscapes that evoke an eerie stillness. (figure 1) Examples of Bell's early work (figures 2 and 3) fall into this category. Tonal in nature, these works clearly show the influence of Harrison. In 1909, Harrison wrote a popular book, *Landscape Painting*, outlining his theories on sensitive American tonalist writings from 1900-1909 on landscape painting. For many years this text became an important guide for landscape artists, both novice and advanced.

In 1907, John F. Carlson (1875-1947) began teaching at the Art Students League Summer School in Woodstock under Birge Harrison. He became the school's director from 1911-1918. Carlson had become an important teacher whose book, *Elementary Principles of Landscape Painting* (1928), served as a bible for generations of landscape painters. Carlson's vigorous, slashing approach to landscape painting with its blazing sunlight was much different than Harrison's peaceful interpretation of nature. (figure 4)

During these years, "Dolly" Bell continued to visit Woodstock where she eventually became convinced of Carlson's theories. Her work became more like Carlson's, her brushwork more spontaneous and her colors more vibrant. Additionally, Bell became involved

Figure 2- Caroline M. Bell, *Cutchogue Landscape, 1911* oil on board, 18 ½ x 27 in.

Figure 3- Caroline M. Bell, *Corn Shocks, 1912* oil on board, 18 x 27 in.

Figures 2 & 3 - Collection of Michael Boro and John Fontana, courtesy of Wallace Gallery.

with the Woodstock Studio where she began to exhibit and sell her paintings.5. (figures 5 & 6)

Figure 4- John F. Carlson, *Across the Meadow*
18 x 24 in.

In 1913 , Caroline Bell participated in the Art Exhibition for the Benefit of Eastern Long Island Hospital at the Masonic Temple in Greenport with two paintings.6. Interestingly, this exhibition included the participation of a few important artists such as Jules Turcas, Nelson Cooke White, Robert Nisbet and others who lived in nearby Old Lyme, Connecticut. The exhibition also featured paintings by *Peconic Art Colony* members Irving Wiles, Edward August Bell, Orlando Rouland, Charles Bittinger and Gladys Wiles.

Between January 28 and February 9, 1919, Bell exhibited a group of paintings at the MacDowell Club in New York City at 108 West 55th Street.7. Established by Edward MacDowell to promote the visual arts, this venue allowed artists who were beginning to become recognized to exhibit there.   Among the artists who exhibited in this group show were Lydia Floret, Sara M. Hess, Frances Keffer, A. Garfield Learnes, Clara Mamre Norton, Delos Pabner, Jr., L. J. Stone, Frances Hudson Storrs, Agnes Weinrich, Julia M. Wickham and Arthur Young. Immediately following this exhibition at the MacDowell Club, from February 18 through March 2, 1919, paintings by George Bellows, Clarence Chatterton, Robert Henri, Leon Kroll, John Sloan, Gifford and Reynolds Beal were exhibited.

Figure 5- Caroline M. Bell, *Italian Fishing Boats*
oil on canvas board, 8 x 10 in.

It was shortly after this Bell began taking students, both at her studio on Love Lane and on location at some of her favorite painting haunts on eastern Long Island and at Gloucester, Massachusetts. She also aquired the nicknames "Dolly" and "Mama" from fellow painters.

By the early 1920's, Dolly Bell began her lifelong association with Emile Gruppe (1896-1978), himself a former student of Carlson's whom she met in Woodstock. She also began to visit Rockport, Gloucester and Cape Ann, Massachusetts.   Her arrival at these locations was about the same time as Gruppe's as on the reverse of a

Figure 6- Caroline M. Bell, *Woman on a Path*
oil on board, 4 ¼ x 6 in.

11

painting titled, *Bass Rocks, Rockport*, is a handwritten memo, *"Mama at Straitsmouth Inn, Rockport, Saturday, July 30-Monday, August 8, 1927."*8. Other *Peconic Bay Impressionists* who traveled to these fishing villages with Bell were Julia M. Wickham, Helen Kroeger (Kurth), Otto Kurth, Marguerite Moore Hawkins, Clara Moore Howard, Annie Young, Joseph Hallock, Jr., Rachel Beebe, Madeline Bassarear, Dorothy Raynor, Ruth McAdams and others. They stayed at the *Cove Villa, Straitsmouth Inn* and other rooming houses in Rockport.9.

Figure 7- Emile Gruppe, *New England Winter Landscape* 30 x 32 in.

Widely respected for renderings of fishing boats docked at Gloucester and harsh winter scenes, Gruppe founded the *Gruppe School of Art* in Gloucester in the summer of 1940. In 1942, John Carlson and Gruppe began running the school together.

Emile Gruppe became recognized as a painter who used color in an exaggerated manner. His unique method of using grays, purples and whites as well as his use of shadows and moving water became a basis for teaching his students. Eventually, his influence in American art became evident through the hundreds of students he taught. (figures 7 & 8)

Caroline Bell became an early member of the Rockport Art Association, North Shore Arts Association and Gloucester Society of Artists and began to participate in exhibitions at these organizations.10. Like her mentors, she painted busy seaports, expansive landscapes and remote icy inlets, some within minutes of her studio. Her paintings were spontaneous on the spot images in vibrant colors. Her renderings of the solitude of winter streams and busy docks eventually became her trademark and indicated her love for painting out-of-doors in any weather.

In 1928, Caroline Bell participated in an exhibition at the Pen and Brush Club at 16 East 10th Street in New York City with fellow artists Julia Wickham (1866-1952) and Whitney Myron Hubbard (1875-1965).11. This club was established in 1894 in New York City for women artists, writers and craftswomen. At this exhibition both Bell and Wickham exhibited a number of land-scapes, including a group of "Catskill" pictures, while Hubbard showed a variety of landscapes and seascapes from Connecticut and eastern Long Island.

Figure 8- Emile Gruppe, *Gloucester Harbor* oil on canvas, 25 x 30 in.

While staying in Rockport, Bell developed a long friendship with Anthony Thieme (1888-1954).12. Thieme had come to America in 1920 and is one of artists responsible for making Rockport a popular destination for painters. After visiting Rockport for the first time in 1929, he began his legendary *Thieme School of Art on Cape Ann* in 1930. Today, he is considered one of the most important and influential teachers to have lived in the region. (figure 9)

Figure 9- Anthony Thieme, *Fishing Pier,* oil on canvas, 12 x 16 in.

In addition to her painting on the North Fork, Bell visited East Hampton, Long Island. There she painted scenes of the Woodhouse Water Garden, possibly with Gaines Ruger Donoho.13. It is not known how many years Bell rented a house on Route 114 in East Hampton, but she did become a member of Guild Hall Museum where she exhibited at a number of member shows. Other *Peconic Bay Impressionists* who participated in these exhibitions with Bell were Julia Wickham, Ruth McAdams, Agnes Mothersele, Marguerite Moore Hawkins and Clara Moore Howard. They participated in exhibitions during the 1940's and 1950's.

In 1933, Caroline M. Bell became a member of the National Association of Women Painters & Sculptors. She exhibited five times during a six-year period.

On July 17, 1934, Bell participated in an exhibition with the North Fork Art Club at the Home Bureau Room at the Suffolk County Courthouse in Riverhead. There is little information about when this club was formed. However, many *Peconic Bay Impressionists* exhibited, including Howard, Wickham, Hawkins, Mothersele and Virginia Wood Goddard from the Bell circle. Other North Fork artists who participated were Irving Wiles, Edward August Bell, Edith and Henry Prellwitz, Thomas Currie-Bell and two unknown artists, Mrs. Harvey Duryea and Mrs. Electra Goodale.

In 1937, Bell exhibited a number of *North Fork Scenes* at a solo exhibition in Greenport, Long Island.14. Now over the age of sixty, she began receiving more attention as an artist.

In 1940, at the Southold Tercentenary celebration, Caroline Bell exhibited four paintings of Gloucester while *Peconic Colony* artists Edward August Bell, Irving Wiles, Henry and Edith Prellwitz exhibited Peconic scenes.15. *Peconic Bay Impressionists* who exhibited at the Tercentenary exhibition were Julia Wickham, Clara Moore Howard, Ruth McAdams,

Virinia Wood Goddard and Marguerite Moore Hawkins, who was honored as Chairman of the Exhibition. It is at this time Caroline Bell is further recognized as a leader among North Fork artists when her studio is pictured in the Southold Town Tercentenary book and by Ann Hallock Currie-Bell when the historian writes, "*At the end of a little Mattituck lane, a blue-shuttered studio with picturesque roof and chimney belongs to Caroline Bell, and there a group of talented Mattituck and Cutchogue artists often meet for painting together and for charming exhibitions of their work, Julia Wickham, Virginia Wood Goddard, Marguerite Hawkins and Clara Howard.*"16.

The following year, in 1941, Bell participated in an exhibition at the Long Island Federation of Women's Clubs where she won first prize for one of her dock scenes. Other exhibitions she participated in included her participation at the Catherine Lorillard Wolfe Art Club, N.Y. in 1942 and in an exhibition at the Nassau County Art League in 1944. The same year she joined several other *Peconic Bay Impressionists* in an exhibition for the benefit of the World War II effort at the Allied Artists of America at the New York Historical Society with her painting titled, *Low Tide*.17.

Caroline M. Bell at the Garden City Hotel, 1941.

During the 1950's and early 1960's, Dolly Bell participated in member exhibitions at the Parrish Art Museum in Southampton and at the Suffolk Museum at Stony Brook.18. She also exhibited at the Riverhead Art League where she was a founding member. The following year, in 1963, Bell was the subject of a one-person exhibition at the Old Town Arts & Crafts Guild in Cutchogue. By this time, she had become a local celebrity and important fixture on the North Fork of Long Island. The number of her students and fellow painters came and went and eventually they became known as "Dolly's Crowd." Today, these artists are becoming known as the *Peconic Bay Impressionists*.

Caroline Bell died on October 25, 1970, at the age of 96, while confined to a nursing home in Cutchogue.

Terry Wallace
East Hampton, New York

Lady with a Fan
Self-portrait by Caroline Bell, circa 1910.

Photograph of Caroline Bell, circa 1930.
(Courtesy of Ray Nine)

Selected Exhibitions

1913- Art Exhibition for the Benefit of Eastern L.I. Hospital

1919- MacDowell Club

1921- Allied Artists of Long Island

1922- Woodstock Art Association

1923- Allied Artists of Long Island

1923- North Shore Arts Association

1924- Rockport Art Association

1924- North Shore Arts Association

1925- North Shore Arts Association

1925- Woodstock Art Association

1925- Rockport Art Association

1926- North Shore Arts Association

1927- North Shore Arts Association

1927- Allied Artists of Long Island

1928- Pen & Brush Club (Catskill Pictures)

1928- Allied Artists of Long Island

1929- Allied Artists of Long Island

1928- North Shore Arts Association

1928- Rockport Art Association

1929- North Shore Arts Association

1930- Allied Artists of Long Island

1932- North Shore Arts Association

1932- Gloucester Society of Artists

1933- National Association of Women Painters & Sculptors

1933- Gloucester Society of Artists

1933- Grand Central Art Galleries

1934- North Fork Art Club, Riverhead

1934- Gloucester Society of Artists

1934- North Shore Arts Association

1935- Grand Central Art Galleries

1935- National Association of Women Painters & Sculptors

1935- Allied Artists of Long Island

1936- National Association of Women Painters & Sculptors

1936- Allied Artists of Long Island

1936- Gloucester Society of Artists

1936- Grand Central Art Galleries

1937- National Association of Women Painters & Sculptors

1937- North Shore Arts Association

1937- Gloucester Society of Artists

1937-"North Fork Scenes" Greenport Methodist Church, Greenport

1938- North Shore Arts Association

1938- Gloucester Society of Artists

1938- National Association of Women Painters & Sculptors

1940-Southold Tercentenary Exhibition (4 paintings Gloucester)

1941- North Shore Arts Association

1941- Long Island Federation of Women's Clubs (First Prize)

1941- Nassau County Art League

1942- Catherine Lorillard Wolfe Art Club, N.Y. (Annual exhibition)

1944- Nassau County Art League

1944- Gloucester Society of Artists

1944- Allied Artists of America at NY Historical Society

1945- Long Island Artists Award Exhibition (Suffolk Museum at Stony Brook)

1946- Nassau County Art League

1947- Long Island Artists Award Exhibition (Suffolk Museum at Stony Brook)

1948- Long Island Artists Award Exhibition (Suffolk Museum at Stony Brook)

1950- Members Exhibition Guild Hall Museum, East Hampton

1951- North Shore Arts Association

1951- Long Island Artists Award Exhibition (Suffolk Museum at Stony Brook)

1952- Long Island Artists Award Exhibition (Suffolk Museum at Stony Brook)

1952- Members Exhibition Guild Hall Museum, East Hampton

1953- North Shore Arts Association

1954- Gloucester Society of Artists

1953- Members Exhibition Guild Hall Museum, East Hampton

1954- Annual Art Festival, Parrish Art Museum, Southampton

1954- Members Exhibition Guild Hall Museum, East Hampton

1956- Members Exhibition Guild Hall Museum, East Hampton

1957- Annual Art Festival, Parrish Art Museum, Southampton

1958- Annual Art Festival, Parrish Art Museum, Southampton

1959- Annual Art Festival, Parrish Art Museum, Southampton

1960- Members Exhibition Guild Hall Museum, East Hampton

1962- Annual Art Festival, Parrish Art Museum, Southampton

1962- Riverhead Art League

1963- Members Exhibition Guild Hall Museum, East Hampton

1963- Old Town Arts & Crafts Guild Exhibition (featured artist), Cutchogue, LI

1964- Annual Art Festival, Parrish Art Museum, Southampton

1970- Dolly Bell Memorial Exhibition, Mattituck Public Library

1976- Caroline Bell Retrospective, Mattituck Public Library

1994- Guild Hall Museum (The Artist as Teacher: Chase and Irving Wiles)

1995- Museums at Stony Brook (Henry & Edith Mitchill Prellwitz)

1996- U.S. Federal Reserve Exhibition (Henry & Edith Mitchill Prellwitz)

2000-Southold Historical Society ("Dolly Bell and Friends")

2006-Wallace Gallery, East Hampton, N.Y. (Caroline M. Bell and The Peconic Bay Impressionists)

2006-Suffolk County Historical Society (Caroline M. Bell and The Peconic Bay Impressionists)

Memberships

Allied Artists of America
Allied Artists of Long Island
Gloucester Society of Artists
Guild Hall Museum
Nassau County Art League
National Association of Women Painters & Sculptors
North Fork Art Club
North Shore Arts Association
Old Town Arts & Crafts Guild
Parrish Art Museum
Riverhead Art League
Rockport Art Association
Suffolk Museum at Stony Brook
Woodstock Art Association

Caroline "Dolly" Bell instructing Peconic Bay Impressionists, circa 1930.
(Courtesy of Ray Nine)

1. *Winter Day, Cutchogue, 1917*
Oil on board, 17 ½ x 27 inches. Signed lower left, dated 1917.

2. *Haystacks, New Suffolk*
Oil on board, 18 ½ x 27 inches. Signed verso.

3. *Sheep Herd*
Oil on board, 18 ¼ x 27 inches. Signed lower left.

4. *Silence of Winter*
Oil on board, 11 x 13 inches. Signed lower left.

5. *Golden Winter*
Oil on board, 18 ⅜ x 27 inches. Unsigned.

6. *Quiet Morning, Gloucester, 1946*
Oil on board, 20 x 27 ¾ inches. Signed lower left, dated 1946.

7. *Bass Rocks, Rockport*
Oil on board, 14 x 16 inches. Signed lower left.

8. *High and Dry*
Oil on canvas board, 16 x 12 inches. Unsigned.

9. *White Skiff, Mattituck*
Oil on board, 18 x 20 inches. Signed lower right.

10. *At the Lake*
Oil on board, 18 x 20 inches. Signed lower left.

11. *Catboats*
Oil on board, 11 x 13 inches. Signed verso.

12. *Frozen Creek*
Oil on board, 16 x 20 inches. Signed lower left & right.

13. *Fall, Cutchogue*
Oil on board, 17 ¾ x 19 ½ inches. Signed lower left.

14. *Hilltop View, Gloucester*
Oil on board, 14 x 16 inches. Signed lower right.

15. *Dry Dock*
Oil on canvas, 16 x 20 inches. Signed lower left.

16. *Fall Morning, Laurel Lake, 1936*
Oil on canvas, 20 x 24 inches. Signed lower right, dated 1936.

17. *Street in Amagansett, (William Hand House)*
Oil on board, 18 x 20 inches. Signed lower left.

18. *Cauliflower Patch*
Oil on board, 16 x 20 inches. Signed lower left.

19. *View of Long Beach, Orient*
Oil on board, 11 x 13 inches. Unsigned.

20. *Thicket at Orient*
Oil on board, 11 x 13 inches. Unsigned.

21. *Summer Sketch*
Oil on board, 11 x 13 inches. Signed lower left.

22. *Winter Afternoon*
Oil on board, 10 ½ x 12 ¾ inches. Signed lower left.

23. *Row Boat, Gloucester*
Oil on board, 18 x 20 inches. Signed lower left.

24. *Winter Boathouses*
Oil on canvas board, 14 x 17 inches. Unsigned.

25. *Sloops at Dock*
Oil on canvas board, 16 x 12 inches. Signed lower left.

26. *Winter Shadows*
Oil on canvas, 18 x 20 inches. Signed lower left.

27. *The Hay Boat*
Oil on canvas, 18 x 22 inches. Signed lower left.

28. *Spring Day*
Oil on canvas, 20 x 24 inches. Signed lower left.

29. *Mending Nets*
Oil on canvas board, 20 x 16 inches. Signed lower left.

30. *View of Rocky Neck, Gloucester, ca. 1925*
Oil on canvas board, 16 x 20 inches. Signed lower left.

31. *Summer Landscape*
Oil on board, 16 x 20 inches. Signed lower left.

32. *Afternoon at the Lake*
Oil on board, 16 x 20 inches. Unsigned.

33. *Aquebogue Farm*
Oil on canvas board, 16 x 12 inches. Signed verso.

34. *Gray Day, Gloucester*
Oil on board, 16 x 20 inches. Signed lower left.

35. *Fall Day*
Oil on board, 12 x 16 inches. Signed lower left.

36. *Spring*
Oil on board, 16 x 20 inches. Unsigned.

37. *The Old Barn*
Oil on board, 18 x 20 inches. Signed lower left.

38. *Winter Path*
Oil on board, 12 x 16 inches. Signed lower right.

39. *Winter Stream*
Oil on board, 16 x 13 ¾ inches. Signed lower left.

40. *Low Tide*
Oil on board, 20 x 18 inches. Signed lower left.

41. *Catskill Landscape*
Oil on canvas board, 12 x 16 inches. Unsigned.

42. *At the Dock*
Oil on board, 20 x 16 inches. Signed lower left.

43. *Along the Docks, Greenport*
Oil on board, 20 x 16 inches. Signed lower left.

44. *Calm Sea*
Oil on board, 16 x 12 inches. Signed lower right.

45. *Winter, Mattituck Creek*
Oil on canvas board, 17 ¾ x 20 inches. Unsigned.

46. *Across the Bay* (*Amagansett Ice House*)
Oil on canvas, 20 x 24 inches. Signed lower left.

47. *Winter Landscape, Mattituck*
Oil on board, 12 x 16 inches. Signed lower right.

48. *Dock at Southold*
Oil on canvas board, 24 x 20 inches. Signed lower left.

49. *Iris Garden, Woodhouse Garden, East Hampton*
Oil on panel, 15 ½ x 18 ½ inches. Signed verso.

50. *Inlet Rocks, Mattituck*
Oil on canvas, 18 x 22 inches. Signed lower left.

51. *Winter Creek, Mattituck*
Oil on board, 16 x 20 inches. Signed lower left.

52 . *Greenport Docks*
Oil on board, 16 x 20 inches. Signed lower left.

53. *Carpenter Street, Greenport*
Oil on board, 18 x 20 inches. Signed lower left.

54. *Morning, Gloucester*
Oil on canvas board, 18 x 20 inches. Signed lower left.

55. *Winter Inlet, Mattituck*
Oil on board, 12 x 15 ¾ inches. Signed verso.

56. *Winter Sunset*
Oil on board, 12 x 16 inches. Signed lower left.

At the end of a little Mattituck lane, a blue-shuttered studio with picturesque roof and chimney belongs to Caroline Bell, and there a group of talented Mattituck and Cutchogue artists often meet for painting together and for charming exhibitions of their work, Julia Wickham, Virginia Wood Goddard, Marguerite Hawkins and Clara Howard.[16]

Ann Hollock Currie-Bell
Southold Tercentenary Publication
1939

Caroline M. Bell studio, Love Lane & Sound Avenue, Mattituck.
(Published in Southold Tercentenary Catalogue, 1939)

Dolly's Crowd

Caroline M. Bell and Her Influence on the Peconic Bay Impressionists

Peconic Colony artists Edward August Bell (far left) and Thomas Currie-Bell (far right) with Peconic Bay Impressionists (from left) Julia Wickham, Clara Howard, Marguerite Hawkins, Caroline Bell and Virginia Wood Goddard at the Southold Town Tercentenary Exhibition, 1940.
(Courtesy of the Southold Historical Society)

Julia M. Wickham (1866-1952)

Julia Wickham must be considered a key member of the *Peconic Bay Impressionists*. It is known she and Caroline Bell painted together in the Catskill's in the early 1900's. Furthermore, the pair exhibited together at both the MacDowell Club in 1919 and at the Pen & Brush Club in 1928 with Whitney Hubbard.[19] Additionally, they also participated together in exhibitions at the National Association of Women Painters & Sculptors in the 1930's. Wickham attended college at Mount Holyoke in Western Massachusetts. She was the daughter of William Wickham, the District Attorney of Suffolk County. Stylistically, both Wickham and Bell almost mirrored each other as their careers progressed. Their earliest paintings were tonal in nature, while their later work was rendered in an impressionist manner. Both women were important members of their respective communities. Julia Wickham was the co-founder of the Cutchogue Free Library with her sister-in-law and sometime painting partner Cora Wickham Sibley (1884-1976), while Bell often donated her time and money to a variety of fund raising activities on Long Island.

Afterglow

Oil on board, 18 x 27 inches.   Signed lower left.
Exhibition label National Assn. Women Painters & Sculptors verso.

Autumn Landscape, L. I.
Oil on board, 18 x 27 inches.   Signed lower right.
Exhibition labels Guild Hall, Museums at Stony Brook, 1995
& Grand Central Art Galleries verso.

Winter Landscape, Cutchogue, L.I.
Oil on board, 17 ½ x 21 ½ inches. Signed lower left.

At Orient
Oil on canvas, 16 x 20 inches. Signed lower left.

Portrait of Julia Wickham
by Caroline Bell, circa 1935.

Carrie Carter Wells (1867-1950)

Carrie Carter Wells or Carrie Lucinda Carter as she was named at birth was born in Freeport, Long Island in 1867. She married Charles Wells (1866-1941) and moved to Mattituck, Long Island. Here she became a close friend of Caroline M. Bell, often participating in exhibitions with other *Peconic Bay Impressionists* at the Bell studio on Love Lane. At some unknown time, Carrie Carter Wells moved to St. Augustine, Florida where she painted Florida subjects and became involved with the art colony there.20. She died in 1950 and is buried in New Bethany cemetery in Mattituck, Long Island as are many of the other painters, including Dolly Bell.

Peconic Bay, 1922
Oil on board, 8 x 12 inches. Signed and titled verso.

Virginia Hargraves Wood Goddard (1873-1941)

A portrait painter and frequent visitor to the Bell studio, Virginia Hargraves Wood Goddard painted the portraits of many influential people during the early part of the 20th century. Born in Washington, D.C., she studied with William Merritt Chase and in Europe. Her brother Waddy Wood was one of the leading architects and designers in the nation. One must wonder if her painting of Gertrude Stein, one of the most important patrons and authorities on art in the early twentieth century was rendered when the sitter was visiting eastern Long Island.

Portrait of Gertrude Stein
Oil on canvas, 14 x 12 inches. Signed lower right, title verso.

Whitney Myron Hubbard (1875-1965)

Whitney Hubbard and Dolly Bell painted together on numerous occasions throughout their lives. Their love of painting out-of-doors and being around other artists was their common bond. Hubbard graduated from Wesleyan University and studied with Frank Vincent DuMond at the Art Students League. He had numerous one-man exhibitions during his lifetime. The head of the art department at the Suffolk Conservatory of Music and Art, Hubbard must be considered a major influence in the Peconic art scene as he taught dozens of artists including Franklin Bennett (Born 1908), Joseph Beckwith Hartranft (1890-1982), Emily Barto (1896-1968), Rachel Beebe (1897-1996), Harold A. Hedges (1932-1995) and George Hallock (1916-1984).

Bluffs at Greenport, Long Island
Oil on canvas, 30 x 36 inches. Signed lower left.

Marguerite Moore Hawkins (1881-1956)

Marguerite Moore Hawkins was married to Charles Percy Hawkins (1879-1958), an important figure in Suffolk County politics. She and her husband resided at Manor Hill in Cutchogue. They also lived for a time at 343 State Street in Albany, New York where she painted and participated in art exhibitions.[21.] Hawkins and Caroline Bell were close friends and painting partners for many years. They often traveled together to the South Fork of Long Island and to Gloucester, Massachusetts where they attended painting classes with Emile Gruppe and Anthony Thieme. Hawkins participated in numerous exhibitions with Dolly Bell and the *Peconic Bay Impressionists* at venues such as Guild Hall, Suffolk Museum at Stony Brook and at the Parrish Art Museum in Southampton. A charter member of the Old Town Arts & Crafts Guild, she helped organize exhibitions there. In 1938, Marguerite Hawkins was appointed Chairman of the Art Exhibit at the Southold Town Tercentenary.

Looking Back, Clarksville
Oil on canvas, 14 x 16 inches. Signed, addressed, Manor Hill/Cutchogue verso.

Before the Race, Peconic Bay, L.I., 1946
Oil on board, 15 ½ x 19 ½ inches. Signed & dated lower right. Title verso.

In The Race, 1943. Southold Yacht Club members test their skill during the club's annual August races.
In the left foreground is the Bluebell, owned by painter Thomas Currie-Bell (1873-1946).
(Courtesy of Southold Historical Society)

Clara Moore Howard (Fitzpatrick) (1882-1961)

Clara Moore Howard was the daughter of George Henry Howard (1848-1936) and Eva Reeve Howard (1854-1939). She lived for most of her life on the family homestead on Love Lane, steps from the Bell studio. Clara M. Howard married local realtor Arthur J. Fitzpatrick in 1948.22. She was a cousin of Marguerite Moore Hawkins, who was a close friend and painting companion. Howard participated in many exhibitions with Caroline Bell and other *Peconic Bay Impressionists* at Guild Hall, East Hampton, Suffolk Museum at Stony Brook, Parrish Art Museum, Southampton, and at the Bell Studio. She was a charter member of the Old Town Arts & Crafts Guild, Cutchogue where she participated in exhibitions with other members of the group. She also partook in the Southold Tercentenary exhibition. She may have been a relation of Lucille Howard, an important female artist and member of *The Philadelphia Ten*, who occasionally visited the North Fork of Long Island.

Yacht at Gloucester
Oil on canvas board, 20 x 16 inches. Signed lower left, title verso.

Autumn Landscape
Oil on canvas board, 18 x 20 inches. Signed lower right.

Sailing in the Peconic
Oil on canvas, 24 x 30 inches. Signed lower left.

Greenport Dock
Oil on masonite, 18 x 20 inches. Signed lower right, title verso.

Clara M. Howard painting at Greenport, circa 1940.
(Courtesy of Mattituck Public Library)

Otto J. Kurth (1883-1965)

Otto Kurth was born in Munich, Germany in 1883. He came to America in 1905 and worked in the Art Department of the New York Times during WWI until 1924. As the Assistant Art Director for Liberty Magazine for 26 years, he worked as a photo engraver.[23] Kurth began spending summers on the North Fork in the 1930's where he met Helen Kroeger. There they opened the *Anchorage Studio* on Marlene Lane in Mattituck. A close friend and painting companion of Dolly Bell, Kurth was closely associated with the Old Town Arts & Crafts Guild of the North Fork. In 1959, the American Photo Engravers selected an oil painting of the Mattituck Presbyterian Church to reproduce on the cover of their December 1959 magazine.[24] This same painting was used as a Christmas card sold by the ladies of the church. In 1962, he won first place at the Riverhead Art League, while his wife Helen Kroeger was awarded second place. Kurth was a member of the Salmagundi Club and the American Artists Professional League.

Misty Harbor, Gloucester
Oil on board, 20 x 16 inches. Signed lower left, title verso.

The Veteran Oak
Oil on canvas board, 16 x 20 inches. Signed lower right.
Anchorage Studio label with title verso.

Reeves Creek, Mattituck, July 1959
Oil on canvas board, 16 x 20 inches. Signed lower right, title verso.

Southold on the Sound, Oct. 1950
Oil on canvas board, 16 x 20 inches. Signed lower right, title verso.

View of Mattituck circa 1935 with location of Bell studio (circled).

The Bell studio, Love Lane, circa 1970.

Cora Billiard Wickham Sibley (1884-1976)

Cora Billiard Wickham Sibley was born in Cutchogue, Long Island. She became the sister-in-law of Julia Wickham after marrying her brother James. After the premature death of her husband in 1914, she married Robert Pelton Sibley. Sibley and her sister-in-law, Julia Wickham were close friends their entire life, sharing the family homestead until 1934. Together, they founded the Cutchogue Free Library. In 1940, Sibley received special mention for her contribution to the Southold Town Tercentenary Book written by Wayland Jefferson, Southold Town Historian. Paintings by Cora Wickham Sibley are rare. Her sketch of the *Old House, Cutchogue* was probably rendered for a local publication.

Old Town House, Cutchogue
Pen and Ink, 8 x 10 inches. Signed & titled verso.
(Courtesy of Southold Historical Society)

Photograph of Old Town House, Cutchogue, circa 1935
(Courtesy of Southold Historical Society)

Franklin Glover Brooks (1886-1955)

Franklin G. Brooks was the older brother of Elliot A. Brooks. He was born in Orient, Long Island and with his brother built a successful commercial fishing business. Sometime later, he moved to Greenport with his wife, Grace. It is believed he painted with Caroline Bell, Madeline Bassarear, Rachel Beebe and other *Peconic Bay Impressionists* from Greenport to Orient sometime in the 1940's.25. He also spent a considerable amount of time painting with his brother, E.A. Brooks. They sold paintings at the General Store in Orient and at Preston's dock in Greenport.

Brown's Beach, Orient, L.I.
Oil on canvas board, 9 x 11 inches. Signed lower left, title verso.

Annie G. Young (1887-1978)

Annie G. Young was a neighbor and close friend of Caroline Bell. She often participated in exhibitions at the Bell studio with other *Peconic Bay Impressionists*. She also accompanied the group on painting excursions along the North Fork and to Gloucester. A charter member of the Old Town Arts & Crafts Guild, Annie Young participated in exhibitions at the Suffolk Museum at Stony Brook, Parrish Art Museum and Guild Hall in East Hampton. Young skillfully utilizes curving paths as a device used to gain depth in her paintings, a theory Caroline Bell learned from her mentor, John Carlson. A technique, Dolly Bell convincingly passed on to her student.

Greenport Street

Oil on canvas board, 16 x 20 inches. Signed lower left. Title reverse with artist's address.

Sound Shore, Mattituck
Oil on canvas board, 18 x 20 inches. Signed & titled verso.

The Farm Road
Oil on canvas board, 16 x 20 inches. Signed lower right, title verso.

Elliot Alvah Brooks (1888-1949)

Elliot A. Brooks was born in Orient, Long Island and lived in the small village for his entire life. He began studying art on his own after possibly being introduced to painting by William Steeple Davis, Harry Roseland or James Knox, all living in Orient. Initially, he painted small marine paintings. Eventually, he skillfully executed local landscapes and seascapes. He occasionally painted with Caroline Bell, Annie Young, Clara Howard, Madeline Bassarear, Marguerite Hawkins and Rachel Beebe as these artists often traveled to Orient.26.

Stormy Surf, Orient, Long Island
Oil on canvas board, 16 x 20 inches. Signed lower right, title verso.

Clara Wells Howell (1888-1976)

Clara Wells Howell was born in Riverhead, Long Island. She lived at 526 East Main Street with her husband Robert Howell. She took painting instruction from Dolly Bell in the 1930's, often painting from Riverhead to Orient Point with her mentor. While it is unknown if she ever traveled to New England with Bell and other *Peconic Bay Impressionists*, it is known she lived in Riverhead her entire life, dying there in 1976. Howell participated in exhibitions at the Bell studio in Mattituck and at the Riverhead Art League in Riverhead. She often sold her paintings in the window at McCabe's store, not far from her home.[27].

The Long Island Sound at Roanoke Landing, 1953
Oil on canvas board, 10 x 14 inches. Signed lower left, dated 1953.
Artist's address & exhibition label verso.

Joseph Beckwith Hartranft (1890-1982)

An artist who shared a love of painting *en plein aire*, Uncle Joe as he was referred to or Joseph Beckwith Hartranft joined Caroline Bell, Julia Wickham, Whitney Hubbard, Marguerite Hawkins, Clara Howard and other *Peconic Bay Impressionists* for painting excursions along the North Fork. A former executive with Devoe Reynolds Paints, Hartranft was the son of a much loved country doctor. He began painting full-time after his retirement. Hartranft, who had a love for sailing, is said to have painted some 2000 paintings of the North Fork of Long Island.[28]. He was the leader of the *Tuesday Art Club* with founding members Larry Waitz, George McAdams, John Kaelin and Gilbert Miner.[29].

Late Snow, 1937
Oil on panel, 5 x 7 inches. Signed lower left, dated 3 April 1937 verso.

Twisted Trees
Oil on canvas, 20 x 24 inches.   Signed lower right.

The Robert Hempstead (Hartranft) House
Oil on canvas, 18 x 20 inches. Signed verso.

Madeline Horton Bassarear (1891-1988)

Madeline Bassarear was a skilled landscape painter and long-time friend of Caroline Bell. She participated in many exhibitions and gatherings at the Bell studio with other *Peconic Bay Impressionists*. A member of the Old Town Arts & Crafts Guild, Bassarear lived for at least part of her life in Greenport, Long Island. Bassarear was a member of the *Tuesday Art Club* with Joseph Beckwith Hartranft, Larry Waitz, George McAdams, John Kaelin, Gil Miner and others.[30]. Her painting, *Mallard Inn, East Marion* is a rendering of a popular dining spot once standing on the southwest side of the causeway as you proceed east to Orient. The Inn closed sometime in the late 1950's or early 1960's. A modern house now occupies this real estate. Perhaps, Bassarear painted this local establishment for posterity.

Mallard Inn, East Marion, L.I., circa 1940
Oil on board, 15 ¾ x 19 ¾ inches. Signed lower left, title verso.

View Near The Inlet
Oil on board, 15 ¾ x 20 inches. Signed lower left.

Caroline M. Bell (left) with Madeline Bassarear, circa 1950.
(Courtesy of Ray Nine)

Helen M. Kroeger Kurth (1892-1986)

Like her husband, Otto Kurth, Helen Kroeger was trained as an illustrator. With him, she opened the *Anchorage Studio* in Mattituck. Kroeger and her husband became close friends and painting partners with Dolly Bell and often participated in exhibitions at the Bell studio on Love Lane. They also participated in exhibitions at the Old Town Arts & Crafts Guild, Parrish Art Museum and Guild Hall, East Hampton. Together, the Kurth's traveled with Bell and the *Peconic Bay Impressionists* to New England and rented rooms at the Straitsmouth Inn, Gloucester where the group often stayed. In 1960, Helen Kroeger and her husband moved to Mattituck permanently. She died there in 1986.

Sound Bluffs
Oil on canvas board, 16 x 20 inches. Signed lower left, title verso.

March Wind & Sunlight
Oil on canvas board, 16 x 20 inches. Signed lower right.
Anchorage Studio label verso with title.

Originally a real estate office where the Hess gas station is now located, this small building was moved to Marlene Lane in the 1950's where it became the Anchorage Studio for Helen Kroeger and Otto Kurth. Pictured is the studio as it appears today.

Kroeger-Kurth House during renovation, circa 1980.
(Courtesy Mark and Ann Gaynor)

Rachel Beebe (1897-1996)

Rachel Beebe lived in Greenport, L.I. for most of her life where she raised her four children by herself. She began painting in the 1940's, attending classes with Whitney Hubbard. She also traveled to Maine where she studied watercolor painting with Edgar Albert Whitney (1891-1987). As a result of this training, she became an accomplished watercolorist. Beebe joined Caroline Bell, Madeline Bassarear, Clara Moore Howard and other *Peconic Bay Impressionists* for painting excursions to Gloucester, Massachusetts.31. They also painted together along the docks in Greenport near Beebe's home. Each summer, Beebe participated in a show at Preston's dock in Greenport with other members of the group. There they sold paintings for little money. She died just shy of her 100th birthday in 1996. In 1997, Beebe was the subject of a major retrospective at the Island Artists Gallery in Greenport.

Dry Dock, Greenport, L.I.
Oil on board, 12 x 16 inches. Signed lower right.

Agnes J. Mothersele (1898-1977)

A descendant of Southold Town founder, Rev. John Youngs, Agnes Mothersele was hailed as *"one of the best known and best liked women of Southold"* in a news article which was published shortly after her death. Mothersele was often referred to as a *"Renaissance Woman"* within the community.[32] She was one of the founders of the Old Town Arts and Crafts Guild in Cutchogue and was the first president. Besides being an artist, Agnes Mothersele was involved with the theatre where she was an accomplished set designer. She served three terms as President of the Cutchogue library and was on the board of the Cutchogue-New Suffolk Historical Council. An avid golfer, Mothersele won the first women's championship at the North Fork Country Club. With Dolly Bell and other *Peconic Bay Impressionists*, she painted along the quiet roads and tranquil seaside surrounding Southold Town. Mothersele participated in exhibitions at the Suffolk Museum at Stony Brook, Parrish Art Museum and at Guild Hall in East Hampton. At the 6th Annual Award Exhibition in 1951, held at the Suffolk Museum in Stony Brook, Mothersele received first prize for her marine painting, *Earth's Ramparts*.[33] She was the subject of a major retrospective at the Cutchogue-New Suffolk Free Library in 2006.

Watching the Race, Peconic Bay, circa 1940
Oil on board, 18 x 20 inches Signed verso.

Self-portrait of Agnes J. Mothersele
Oil on canvas, 20 x 16 inches. Signed verso.

New Suffolk
Oil on canvas, 20 x 24 inches. Signed and titled verso.

Ruth McAdams (1901-1972)

Ruth McAdams studied art at the Pratt Institute in Brooklyn, New York. She also took instruction from Caroline M. Bell and Gladys Wiles Jepson (1894-1984). McAdams was a founding member of the Old Town Arts & Crafts Guild in Cutchogue. She traveled with Bell and the *Peconic Bay Impressionists* to Gloucester, Massachusetts.[34] McAdams was a frequent visitor to the Bell studio on Love Lane in Mattituck and took part in exhibitions there. She exhibited with the group at the Suffolk Museum at Stony Brook and at the Parrish Art Museum, Southampton.

Smiling Fields, Nassau Point
Oil on canvas board, 12 x 14 ¾ inches. Signed lower left & titled verso.

Story of Vermeer, 1922
Oil on canvas, 22 x 19 inches. Signed lower right, artist's address verso.

*Straitsmouth Inn, Gloucester, circa 1930, where Caroline Bell and the
Peconic Bay Impressionists often stayed.*

*Caroline Bell (center) with Peconic Bay Impressionists at
Gloucester, Mass. circa 1935.*

John H. Kaelin (1901-1990)

John H. Kaelin was born in Cutchogue, Long Island. He began painting late in life, studying with Joseph Beckwith Hartranft. A long-time member of the Old Town Arts & Crafts Guild in Cutchogue, he received public recognition for his painting. Kaelin was a founding member of the *Tuesday Art Club* with Hartranft, Gilbert B. Miner, George McAdams and Larry Waitz. He occasionally travelled to Rockport, Mass. with Miner where they painted with Emile Gruppe and other Rockport artists.[35]

Harbor, New Suffolk
Oil on canvas board, 12 x 16 inches. Signed lower right & titled verso.

Dorothy E. Raynor (1905-1972)

Dorothy E. Raynor was a trained archeologist who became a friend and student of Caroline Bell in the thirties. She participated in exhibitions and social gatherings at the Bell studio until Dolly Bell died in 1970. "Dot" Raynor, as she was affectionately known, was a member of the Old Town Arts & Craft Guild in Cutchogue where she participated in exhibitions. She also travelled with the *Peconic Bay Impressionists* to Gloucester, Massachusetts. A charter member and president of the Long Island Chapter of the New York State Archeological Association, Dorothy Raynor is interned at the Eastport Bible Church, Main Street, Eastport, Long Island.[36].

View of the Bluffs
Oil on canvas board, 10 x 14 inches. Signed lower left.

George McAdams (Born 1906)

George McAdams was the younger brother of Ruth McAdams. He was born in Brooklyn, New York where he attended figure drawing classes at Pratt Institute.[37] Shortly after World War II, he began painting landscapes on a regular basis. He studied with Joseph Beckwith Hartranft and Madeline Bassarear. McAdams was a founding member of the *Tuesday Art Club* with Hartranft, John Kaelin, Gilbert Miner and Larry Waitz. As a result of his education at the Pratt Institute, McAdams became a skilled draftsman. He also occasionally made wooden toys and sculptures.

Cedar Beach, Southold
Oil on canvas, 16 x 20 inches. Signed lower left & titled verso.

Franklin Bennett (Born 1908)

Franklin Bennett hailed from East Marion, Long Island. He was the younger brother of painter, Joseph H. Bennett (1889-1989) who lived in California. Bennett eventually followed his older brother to the West Coast where he became involved with other artists in the Oakland area. As a young man, Franklin Bennett studied with Whitney Hubbard and Caroline Bell. Bennett briefly accompanied the *Peconic Bay Impressionists* on painting excursions. He also participated in an exhibition at the National Arts Club where he won a prize in 1928.[38].

Winter Shadows, 1927
Oil on board, 8 x 10 inches. Signed lower right, dated 1927.

Albert Latham (1909-1976)

Albert Latham was born in Orient, Long Island where he lived his entire life. He was a skilled carpenter who began painting as a hobby. Latham probably began his art career painting with the Brooks brothers, as his early style of painting and subject matter was similar to theirs. He also occasionally painted with Madeline Bassarear and Rachel Beebe.[39.] He became a skilled palette knife artist, possibly learning the technique from Caroline Bell. Latham often taught palette knife painting classes in Orient. Among his students were Larry Waitz and several other early members of the *Tuesday Art Club*.[40.]

The Scallop Fleet, Peconic Bay
Oil on canvas board, 18 x 24 inches. Signed lower right.

Gilbert B. Miner (1910-1999)

A graduate of Oswego State Teachers College with a master's degree from New York University, Miner came to Southold in 1942. There he taught industrial arts at Southold High School. A founding member of the Old Town Arts & Crafts Guild in Cutchogue with Agnes Mothersele, George W. Hallock, Jr., Caroline Bell, Annie Young, Marguerite Hawkins and other artists, he joined Joseph Beckwith Hartranft, John H. Kaelin, George McAdams and Larry Waitz on Tuesdays, forming the *Tuesday Art Club*. This group of artists first began meeting at the Indian Museum in Southold where they painted out-of-doors and critiqued each other's work. Over the years, this club grew to include Frances Moran, Ann Razzo, Adelaide O'Connell, Rose Hutchinson, Mary Murtagh, Ruth Hammell, John Stack and other local artists.41.

Waterfront, New Suffolk
Oil on canvas board, 16 x 20 inches. Signed lower right & titled verso.

Josephine M. Brooks (1910-2002)

Josephine M. Brooks was a painter of landscapes and seascapes. Born in 1910, she began her studies with Dolly Bell in the 1950's after Bell had gained prominence in the community. It is a possibility Josephine Brooks was a relative of the Brooks brothers who hailed from Orient Point. *Rocks on the Sound* was skillfully executed with a palette knife, clearly showing the influence and style of Albert Latham who she may have painted with.

Rocks on the Sound
Oil on canvas board, 12 x 16 inches. Signed lower right.

Larry Waitz (Born 1910)

A veterinarian by profession, Larry Waitz began painting in the early 1960's. He studied with Joseph Beckwith Hartranft, Helen Kroeger, Dorothy Raynor and Albert Latham.42. A member of the Old Town Arts & Crafts Guild in Cutchogue for approximately 40 years where he often exhibited, Waitz was a founding member of the *Tuesday Art Club*. Later in life, he became an award winning watercolorist. His wife, Ann Mears Waitz was an accomplished author.

Peconic Landscape
Oil on canvas board, 8 x 10 inches. Signed lower left.

Florence Sidbury Kramer (Born 1915)

Florence Sidbury Kramer studied fashion design in New York City with Ethel Traphagen at the Traphagen School of Design. After marrying John J. Kramer, she moved to Southold, Long Island. In the 1940's, she took up painting, studying with Whitney Hubbard and Gladys Wiles. Shortly after this, she began painting with Caroline Bell, Agnes Mothersele and other *Peconic Bay Impressionists*. After the death of her husband, Florence Kramer spent two winters in North Carolina teaching painting at the Cape Fear Technical Institute. Returning to the Peconic region, she set up her studio in Greenport and began taking students. In addition to painting, Kramer also hooked rugs and wrote prose and poetry.[43]

Fishing Smack, Mattituck
Oil on canvas board, 16 x 20 inches Signed lower left.

George W. Hallock, Jr. (1916-1984)

In 1950, George W. Hallock, Jr. became a founding member and one of the first officers of the Old Town Arts and Crafts Guild in Cutchogue. With Agnes J. Mothersele (President), Hallock served as one of the fledgling organization's Vice-Presidents. There he exhibited with other members of the Guild.[44] It is believed George Hallock received his introduction to painting from Whitney Hubbard in the Greenport School District. He also received some instruction from William Steeple Davis, a resident of Orient and an academically trained artist. With Caroline Bell, Mothersele and other *Peconic Bay Impressionists*, he painted out-of-doors from New Suffolk to Orient Point. He also traveled to Gloucester, Massachusetts with members of the group.[45] Sometime during the 1960's, he moved to Merion, Pennsylvania where he began painting in watercolor.

Cloudy Day, Orient, L.I.
Oil on board, 9 x 12 inches. Signed lower left.

Harold A. Hedges (1932-1995)

Harold Hedges was the only child of Henry Hedges and Edna Hand. As a young man, he attended public school in Greenport, Long Island. There he enrolled in art class with Whitney Hubbard. Hedges joined Caroline Bell and other *Peconic Bay Impressionists* on painting excursions along the North Fork of Long Island. *Scene Near The Sound* was rendered at Clark's Beach in Greenport.46.

Scene Near The Sound, 1953
Oil on board, 9 x 12 inches. Signed lower right, date & title verso.

Lewis J. Carpenter (1937-1975)

There is little known about the artist, Lewis J. Carpenter. It is thought he was a student of either Joseph Beckwith Hartranft or Rachel Beebe.47. *Young's Landing* in Orient, Long Island was a favorite subject among *Peconic Bay Impressionists*. This motif is still visible and intact as one is heading east to Orient Point on the south side of the road after entering the causeway in East Marion.

Young's Landing, Orient, L.I., September 11, 1963
Oil on canvas board, 6 x 8 inches. Signed lower right & titled verso.

Working on the first home of the Arts & Crafts Guild in Cutchogue, ca. 1951.
(left to right) Ruth McNish Reinhardt, Eunice Prellwitz, and Agnes Mothersele (president)

Bibliography

American Art Analog, Vol. II. Chelsea House Publishers Inc., New York, NY 1986.

Carlson, John F. "Carlson's Guide to Landscape Painting." Sterling Publishing Co, Inc., New York, 1929.

Currie-Bell, Ann Hallock. "Southold Town Tercentenary Booklet (1626-1939)." Southold Town, Southold, Long Island, 1939.

Esten, John. "Hampton Gardens, a 350 Year Legacy." Rizzoli International Publications, Inc. 2004.

"Exhibition of Landscape and Marine Paintings." Exhibition catalogue: New York Pen & Brush Club, 16 East 10th Street. March 18-31, 1928.

Falk, Peter Hastings. "Who Was Who in American Art, 1564-1975". Soundview Press, Madison, Ct., 1999.

Gerdts, William H. "American Impressionism." The Henry Art Gallery, Univ. of Washington, Seattle, 1980.

"Gloucester Society of Artists." Various exhibition catalogues: Massachusetts. East Gloucester.

"Guild Hall Museum." Various exhibition checklists: New York. Guild Hall, East Hampton.

Jefferson, Wayland. "Old Southold Town's Tercentenary (1640-1940)" Country Life Press, Garden City, NY, 1940.

Kelsey, Carelton. "Main Street Treasures, Carleton Kelsey's Amagansett." Amagansett Historical Society, May 2000.

Kramer, John. "Dolly Bell and Friends: Scenes of the North Fork by Caroline M. Bell & Contemporaries." Exhibition catalogue: New York. Southold Historical Society, March 4-May 7, 2000.

Morley, Arthur P. "Rockport, A Town of the Sea." The Murray Printing Co., Cambridge, Mass., 1924.

"North Shore Arts Association." Various exhibition catalogues: Massachusetts. East Gloucester Square, East Gloucester, Mass.

"Parrish Art Museum." Various exhibition pamphlets & catalogues: New York. Parrish Art Museum, Southampton.

"Photographic History of Gloucester." Volume three. Cape Ann Bank and Trust Co., Gloucester, Mass., 1959.

Pisano, Ronald G. & Cameron, Kate. "The Artist as Teacher: Chase and Irving Wiles." Exhibition catalogue: New York. Guild Hall, East Hampton, 1994.

Pisano, Ronald. "Henry and Edith Mitchell Prellwitz and the Peconic Art Colony." Exhibition catalogue, New York: Museums at Stony Brook, Stony Brook, NY (May13-Sept. 10, 1995), Federal Reserve Board, Washington, D.C. (January 25-March 22, 1996).

_____. "Whitney M. Hubbard, Early 20th Century Painter," Exhibition catalogue: New York. Village of Greenport, L.I., June 2000.

Preato, Robert R., Langer, Sandra. " Impressionism and Post Impressionism." Grand Central Art Galleries, Inc., 1988.

"Rockport Art Association." Various exhibition catalogues: Massachusetts. The Rockport Art Association, Rockport.

Robinson, F.J.G. "Tragabigzanda or Cape Ann: The Romance, Legend and History of Cape Ann, Past & Present," 1935.

Rosenfeld, Alice J. "Caroline M. Bell (1874-1970)." Mattituck Public Library, 1976.

Solley, George. "Alluring Rockport." North Shore Press Inc. Printers. Manchester-by-the-Sea, Mass., 1924.

"Suffolk Museum at Stony Brook." Various exhibition pamphlets: New York. Suffolk Museum, Stony Brook.

Wallace, Terry. " By the Sea, American Paintings of the Northeast Coast." Exhibition catalogue: New York. Wallace Gallery, East Hampton, 1999.

_____. "Fifty Years of American Painting, (1860-1910)." Exhibition catalogue: New York. Wallace Gallery, East Hampton, 2003.

Notes

1. Obituary of Caroline M. Bell in Long Island Traveler, Oct 26, 1970.

2. News article Suffolk Weekly Times newspaper, July 28, 1906.

3. News article Brooklyn Eagle newspaper, Sept. 11, 1887.

4. News article in the Suffolk Weekly Times newspaper, July 14, 1906.

5. This information was obtained by Woodstock Studio exhibition labels on the reverse of small paintings by Caroline Bell.

6. Ronald Pisano points out that artists from both sides of Long Island Sound participated in these exhibitions.

7. The MacDowell Club was established to promote the careers of promising artists. Information of participants in this exhibition were obtained in an exhibition catalogue Jan 28-Feb 19, 1919.

8. This was learned from the notation on the reverse of painting in Dolly Bell's hand with dates.

9. This information was obtained through interviews conducted by Alice Rosenfeld.

10. This information was obtained through various exhibition catalogues.

11. Information obtained from an exhibition catalogue from Pen & Brush Club, 1928.

12. Alice Rosenfeld interviewed several people who painted with Caroline M. Bell. This included Helen Kroeger (Kurth).

13. John Esten wrote extensively about the Woodhouse Water Garden in his book on Long Island gardens. Esten spoke about the similarities of a Caroline Bell painting rendered at the Woodhouse property and a photograph of the same location he obtained from the Smithsonian.

14. This was learned from an article in the Long Island Traveler newspaper.

15. Ann Hallock Currie-Bell, wife of the artist Thomas Currie Bell spoke highly of all of the artists involved in the Tercentenary exhibition published in the Southold Town Tercentenary Book.

16. ibid.

17. This information was learned from an exhibition label from the Allied Artists of America on the verso of *Low Tide*.

18. This information was obtained through numerous exhibition checklists and catalogues published at The Parrish Art Museum, Suffolk County Museum at Stony Brook and Guild Hall Museum.

19. This information was obtained from exhibition catalogues.

20. Obituary of Carrie Carter Wells in Suffolk Weekly Times newspaper, October 5, 1950.

21. Obituary of Charles Percy Hawkins in Suffolk Weekly Times newspaper, January 17, 1958.

22. Obituary of Arthur J. Fitzpatrick in Suffolk Weekly Times newspaper, February 16, 1962.

23. News article in Long Island Traveler, 1965.

24. Obituary of Otto J. Kurth in Suffolk Weekly Times newspaper, March 4, 1965.

25. This was discussed in an interview with Larry Waitz, August 2006.

26. ibid.

27. This was learned from an exhibition label on the reverse of a painting in the artist's hand.

28. News article Peconic Bay Shopper, May 4, 1988.

29. This was discussed in conversations with Larry Waitz and George McAdams in August & September 2006.

30. ibid.

31. This was discussed in an interview with Larry Waitz, August 2006.

32. News article in Suffolk Weekly Times, February 3, 1977.

33. News article in Suffolk Weekly Times, October 7, 1976.

34. This was discussed in an interview with George McAdams, September 2006.

35. This was discussed in conversations with Larry Waitz and George McAdams in August & September 2006.

36. Information obtained from headstone at Eastport Bible Church cemetery, Eastport, L.I.

37. This was discussed in an interview with George McAdams, September 2006.

38. Information obtained in Who was Who in American Art, Vol. I.

39. This was discussed in an interview with Larry Waitz, August 2006.

40. This was discussed in conversations with Larry Waitz and George McAdams in August & September 2006.

41. ibid.

42. This was discussed in an interview with Larry Waitz, August 2006.

43. This was learned from John Kramer, Southold Historical Society, Dolly Bell and Friends, exhibition catalogue, March 4-May 7, 2000.

44. News article Suffolk Weekly Times, February 11, 1952.

45. This was discussed in telephone conversations with George W. Hallock, IV, in July 2006.

46. This was learned from notes on the reverse of a painting in the artist's hand.

47. This was discussed in an interview with Larry Waitz, August 2006.

Caroline M. Bell
Checklist of Paintings

1. *Winter Day, Cutchogue, 1917*
Oil on board, 17 ½ x 27 inches. Signed lower left,
dated 1917.

2. *Haystacks, New Suffolk*
Oil on board, 18 ½ x 27 inches. Signed verso.

3. *Sheep Herd*
Oil on board, 18 ¼ x 27 inches. Signed lower left.

4. *Silence of Winter*
Oil on board, 11 x 13 inches. Signed lower left.

5. *Golden Winter*
Oil on board, 18 ⅜ x 27 inches. Unsigned.

6. *Quiet Morning, Gloucester, 1946*
Oil on board, 20 x 27 ¾ inches. Signed lower left,
dated 1946.

7. *Bass Rocks, Rockport*
Oil on board, 14 x 16 inches. Signed lower left.

8. *High and Dry*
Oil on canvas board, 16 x 12 inches. Unsigned.

9. *White Skiff, Mattituck*
Oil on board, 18 x 20 inches. Signed lower right.

10. *At the Lake*
Oil on board, 18 x 20 inches. Signed lower left.

11. *Catboats*
Oil on board, 11 x 13 inches. Signed verso.

12. *Frozen Creek*
Oil on board, 16 x 20 inches. Signed lower left &
right.

13. *Fall, Cutchogue*
Oil on board, 17 ¾ x 19 ½ inches. Signed lower left.

14. *Hilltop View, Gloucester*
Oil on board, 14 x 16 inches. Signed lower right.

15. *Dry Dock*
Oil on canvas, 16 x 20 inches. Signed lower left.

16. *Fall Morning, Laurel Lake, 1936*
Oil on canvas, 20 x 24 inches. Signed lower right,
dated 1936.

17. *Street in Amagansett, (William Hand House)*
Oil on board, 18 x 20 inches. Signed lower left.

18. *Cauliflower Patch*
Oil on board, 16 x 20 inches. Signed lower left.

19. *View of Long Beach, Orient*
Oil on board, 11 x 13 inches. Unsigned.

20. *Thicket at Orient*
Oil on board, 11 x 13 inches. Unsigned.

21. *Summer Sketch*
Oil on board, 11 x 13 inches. Signed lower left.

22. *Winter Afternoon*
Oil on board, 10 ½ x 12 ¾ inches. Signed lower left.

23. *Row Boat, Gloucester*
Oil on board, 18 x 20 inches. Signed lower left.

24. *Winter Boathouses*
Oil on canvas board, 14 x 17 inches. Unsigned.

25. *Sloops at Dock*
Oil on canvas board, 16 x 12 inches. Signed lower
left.

26. *Winter Shadows*
Oil on canvas, 18 x 20 inches. Signed lower left.

27. *The Hay Boat*
Oil on canvas, 18 x 22 inches. Signed lower left.

28. *Spring Day*
Oil on canvas, 20 x 24 inches. Signed lower left.

29. *Mending Nets*
Oil on canvas board, 20 x 16 inches. Signed lower left.

30. *View of Rocky Neck, Gloucester, ca. 1925*
Oil on canvas board, 16 x 20 inches. Signed lower left.

31. *Summer Landscape*
Oil on board, 16 x 20 inches. Signed lower left.

32. *Afternoon at the Lake*
Oil on board, 16 x 20 inches. Unsigned.

33. *Aquebogue Farm*
Oil on canvas board, 16 x 12 inches. Signed verso.

34. *Gray Day, Gloucester*
Oil on board, 16 x 20 inches. Signed lower left.

35. *Fall Day*
Oil on board, 12 x 16 inches. Signed lower left.

36. *Spring*
Oil on board, 16 x 20 inches. Unsigned.

37. *The Old Barn*
Oil on board, 18 x 20 inches. Signed lower left.

38. *Winter Path*
Oil on board, 12 x 16 inches. Signed lower right.

39. *Winter Stream*
Oil on board, 16 x 13 ¾ inches. Signed lower left.

40. *Low Tide*
Oil on board, 20 x 18 inches. Signed lower left.

41. *Catskill Landscape*
Oil on canvas board, 12 x 16 inches. Unsigned.

42. *At the Dock*
Oil on board, 20 x 16 inches. Signed lower left.

43. *Along the Docks, Greenport*
Oil on board, 20 x 16 inches. Signed lower left.

44. *Calm Sea*
Oil on board, 16 x 12 inches. Signed lower right.

45. *Winter, Mattituck Creek*
Oil on canvas board, 17 ¾ x 20 inches. Unsigned.

46. *Across the Bay (Amagansett Ice House)*
Oil on canvas, 20 x 24 inches. Signed lower left.

47. *Winter Landscape, Mattituck*
Oil on board, 12 x 16 inches. Signed lower right.

48. *Dock at Southold*
Oil on canvas board, 24 x 20 inches. Signed lower left.

49. *Iris Garden, Woodhouse Garden, East Hampton*
Oil on panel, 15 ½ x 18 ½ inches. Signed verso.

50. *Inlet Rocks, Mattituck*
Oil on canvas, 18 x 22 inches. Signed lower left.

51. *Winter Creek, Mattituck*
Oil on board, 16 x 20 inches. Signed lower left.

52. *Greenport Docks*
Oil on board, 16 x 20 inches. Signed lower left.

53. *Carpenter Street, Greenport*
Oil on board, 18 x 20 inches. Signed lower left.

54. *Morning, Gloucester*
Oil on canvas board, 18 x 20 inches. Signed lower left.

55. *Winter Inlet, Mattituck*
Oil on board, 12 x 15 ¾ inches. Signed verso.

56. *Winter Sunset*
Oil on board, 12 x 16 inches. Signed lower left.

Tuesday Art Club member, John H. Kaelin at his easel.
Painted by Larry Waitz at Southold Beach, ca. 1970.

Dolly's Crowd
The Peconic Bay Impressionists

Checklist of Paintings

Julia M. Wickham (1866-1952)

Afterglow
Oil on board, 18 x 27 inches.   Signed lower left.
Exhibition label National Assn. Women Painters &
Sculptors verso.

Autumn Landscape, L. I.
Oil on board, 18 x 27 inches.   Signed lower right.
Exhibition labels Guild Hall, Museums at Stony
Brook, 1995 & Grand Central Art Galleries verso.

Winter Landscape, Cutchogue, L.I.
Oil on board, 17 ½ x 21 ½ inches. Signed lower left.

At Orient
Oil on canvas, 16 x 20 inches. Signed lower left.

Carrie Carter Wells (1867-1950)

Peconic Bay, 1922
Oil on board, 8 x 12 inches. Signed and titled verso.

Virginia Hargraves Wood Goddard (1873-1941)

Portrait of Gertrude Stein
Oil on canvas, 14 x 12 inches. Signed lower right,
title verso.

Whitney Myron Hubbard (1875-1965)

Bluffs at Greenport, Long Island
Oil on canvas, 30 x 36 inches. Signed lower left.

Marguerite Moore Hawkins (1881-1956)

Looking Back, Clarksville
Oil on canvas, 14 x 16 inches. Signed, addressed,
Manor Hill/Cutchogue verso.

Before the Race, Peconic Bay, L.I., 1946
Oil on board, 15 ½ x 19 ½ inches. Signed & dated
lower right. Title verso.

Clara Moore Howard (Fitzpatrick) (1882-1961)

Yacht at Gloucester
Oil on canvas board, 20 x 16 inches. Signed lower
left, title verso.

Autumn Landscape
Oil on canvas board, 18 x 20 inches. Signed lower
right.

Sailing in the Peconic
Oil on canvas, 24 x 30 inches. Signed lower left.

Greenport Dock
Oil on masonite, 18 x 20 inches. Signed lower right,
title verso.

Otto J. Kurth (1883-1965)

Misty Harbor, Gloucester
Oil on board, 20 x 16 inches. Signed lower left, title verso.

The Veteran Oak
Oil on canvas board, 16 x 20 inches. Signed lower
right. Anchorage Studio label with title verso.

Reeves Creek, Mattituck, July 1959
Oil on canvas board, 16 x 20 inches. Signed lower
right, title verso.

Southold on the Sound, Oct. 1950
Oil on canvas board, 16 x 20 inches. Signed lower
right, title verso.

Cora Billiard Wickham Sibley (1884-1976)

Old Town House, Cutchogue
Pen and ink, 8 x 10 inches. Signed & titled verso.

Franklin Glover Brooks (1886-1955)

Brown's Beach, Orient, L.I.
Oil on canvas board, 9 x 11 inches. Signed lower left, title verso.

Annie Young (1887-1978)

Greenport Street
Oil on canvas board, 16 x 20 inches. Signed lower left. Title reverse with artist's address.

Sound Shore, Mattituck
Oil on canvasboard, 18 x 20 inches. Signed & titled verso.

The Farm Road
Oil on canvas board, 16 x 20 inches. Signed lower right, title verso.

Elliot Alvah Brooks (1888-1949)

Stormy Surf, Orient, Long Island
Oil on canvas board, 16 x 20 inches. Signed lower right, title verso.

Clara Wells Howell (1888-1976)

The Long Island Sound at Roanoke Landing, 1953
Oil on canvas board, 10 x 14 inches. Signed lower left, dated 1953. Artist's address & exhibition label verso.

Joseph Beckwith Hartranft (1890-1982)

Late Snow, 1937
Oil on panel, 5 x 7 inches. Signed lower left, dated 3 April 1937 verso.

Twisted Trees
Oil on canvas, 20 x 24 inches. Signed lower right.

The Robert Hempstead (Hartranft) House
Oil on canvas, 18 x 20 inches.   Signed verso.

Madeline Horton Bassarear (1891-1988)

Mallard Inn, East Marion, L.I., circa 1940
Oil on board, 15 ¾ x 19 ¾ inches. Signed lower left, title verso.

View Near The Inlet
Oil on board, 15 ¾ x 20 inches. Signed lower left.

Helen M. Kroeger Kurth (1892-1986)

Sound Bluffs
Oil on canvas board, 16 x 20 inches. Signed lower left, title verso.

March Wind & Sunlight
Oil on canvas board, 16 x 20 inches. Signed lower right. Anchorage Studio label verso with title.

Rachel Beebe (1897-1996)

Dry Dock, Greenport, L.I.
Oil on board, 12 x 16 inches. Signed lower right.

Agnes J. Mothersele (1898-1977)

Watching the Race, Peconic Bay, circa 1940
Oil on board, 18 x 20 inches. Signed verso.

Self-portrait of Agnes J. Mothersele
Oil on canvas, 20 x 16 inches. Signed verso.

New Suffolk
Oil on canvas, 20 x 24 inches. Signed and titled verso.

Ruth McAdams (1901-1972)

Smiling Fields, Nassau Point
Oil on canvas board, 12 x 14 ¾ inches. Signed lower left & titled verso.

Story of Vermeer, 1922
Oil on canvas, 22 x 19 inches. Signed lower right, artist's address verso.

John H. Kaelin (1901-1990)

Harbor New Suffolk
Oil on canvas board, 12 x 16 inches. Signed lower right & titled verso.

Dorothy E. Raynor (1905-1972)

View of the Bluffs
Oil on canvas board, 10 x 14 inches. Signed lower left.

George McAdams (Born 1906)

Cedar Beach, Southold
Oil on canvas board, 16 x 20 inches. Signed lower left & titled verso.

Franklin Bennett (Born 1908)

Winter Shadows, 1927
Oil on board, 8 x 10 inches. Signed lower right, dated 1927.

Albert Latham (1909-1976)

The Scallop Fleet, Peconic Bay
Oil on canvas board, 18 x 24 inches. Signed lower right.

Gilbert B. Miner (1910-1999)

Waterfront, New Suffolk
Oil on canvas board, 16 x 20 inches. Signed lower right & titled verso.

Josephine M. Brooks (1910-2002)

Rocks on the Sound
Oil on canvas board, 12 x 16 inches. Signed lower right.

Larry Waitz (Born 1910)

Peconic Landscape
Oil on canvas board, 8 x 10 inches. Signed lower left.

Florence Sidbury Kramer (Born 1915)

Fishing Smack, Mattituck
Oil on canvas board, 16 x 20 inches. Signed lower left.

George W. Hallock, Jr. (1916-1984)

Cloudy Day, Orient L.I.
Oil on board, 9 x 12 inches. Signed lower left.

Harold A. Hedges (1932-1995)

Scene Near The Sound, 1953
Oil on board, 9 x 12 inches. Signed lower right, date & title verso.

Lewis J. Carpenter (1937-1975)

Young's Landing, Orient, L.I., September 11, 1963
Oil on canvas board, 6 x 8 inches. Signed lower right & titled verso.